T0034491

Author:
Anne Rooney has a PhD in English from the
University of Cambridge. She is the author of
many books for children and adults, specializing
in science and technology topics.

Series creator:
David Salariya was born in Dundee,
Scotland. He has illustrated a wide range of books
and has created and designed many new series
for publishers in the UK and overseas. David
established The Salariya Book Company in 1989.
He lives in Brighton, England, with his wife,
illustrator Shirley Willis, and their son, Jonathan.

Artists:
Alexandre Affonso, Bryan Beach, Jared Green,
Sam Bridges, and Shutterstock.

Editor:
Nick Pierce

© The Salariya Book Company Ltd MMXIX
No part of this publication may be reproduced in whole or in
part, or stored in a retrieval system, or transmitted in any form or
by any means, electronic, mechanical, photocopying, recording,
or otherwise, without written permission of the publisher. For
information regarding permission, write to the copyright holder.

Published in Great Britain in 2019 by
The Salariya Book Company Ltd
25 Marlborough Place, Brighton BN1 1UB

Library of Congress Cataloging-in-Publication Data

Names: Rooney, Anne, author.
Title: The science of seafaring : the float-tastic facts about ships /
   written by Anne Rooney.
Description: New York : Franklin Watts, an imprint of Scholastic Inc., 2019.
   | Series: The science of engineering | Includes index.
Identifiers: LCCN 2018034873| ISBN 9780531131961 (library binding) | ISBN
   9780531133965 (pbk.)
Subjects: LCSH: Ships--Juvenile literature. | Shipbuilding--Juvenile
   literature. | Seafaring life--Juvenile literature.
Classification: LCC VM150 .R6268 2019 | DDC 623.8--dc23 LC

All rights reserved.
Published in 2019 in the United States
by Franklin Watts
An imprint of Scholastic Inc.

Printed and bound in China.
Printed on paper from sustainable sources.
1 2 3 4 5 6 7 8 9 10 R 28 27 26 25 24 23 22 21 20 19

SCHOLASTIC, FRANKLIN WATTS, and associated logos are
trademarks and/or registered trademarks of Scholastic Inc.

This book is sold subject to the
conditions that it shall not, by way of trade or otherwise, be lent,
resold, hired out, or otherwise circulated without the publisher's
prior consent in any form or binding or cover other than that in
which it is published and without similar condition being imposed
on the subsequent purchaser.

PAPER FROM
SUSTAINABLE
FORESTS

The Science of Seafaring

The Float-tastic Facts About Ships

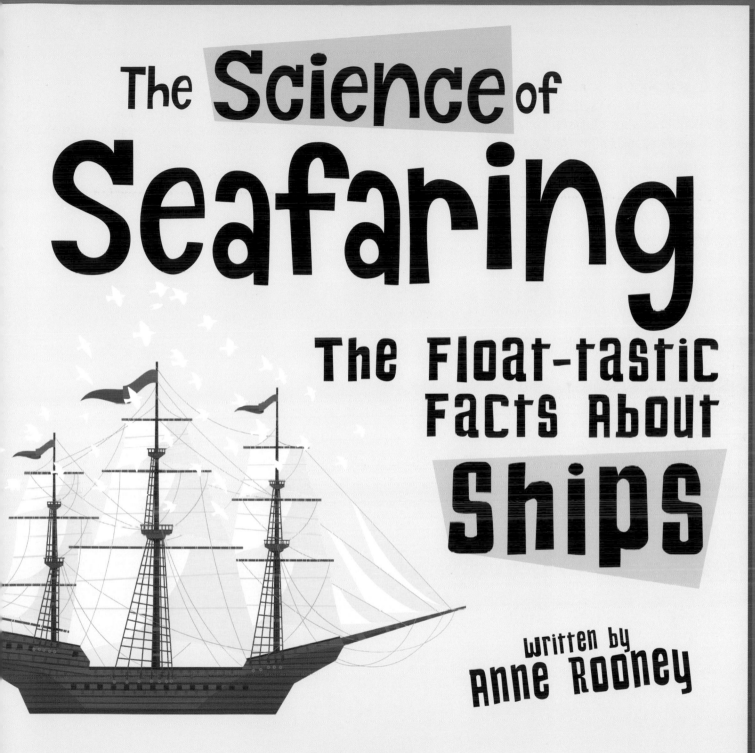

Written by
Anne Rooney

Franklin Watts®
An Imprint of Scholastic Inc.

Contents

Introduction

People have been sailing the sea for thousands of years. Long ago, most seafarers stayed close to the coasts, but some adventurous explorers made awe-inspiring journeys, crossing the oceans to settle in new places. Methods of moving over the sea have changed, from using oars and simple sails to huge powered ships, but the science of seafaring remains the same. The wind, waves, currents, and tides work in the same way. Staying afloat, finding your way, moving through water, and surviving bad weather and other perils are still important to all seafarers, from the lone yachtswoman to the commander of a huge cruise liner.

Hovercraft go over the sea, boats and ships sail through it, and submarines go under the sea. The science of seafaring is the same for all. But some have extra challenges: Submarines have the pressure of water above them, for example.

All at Sea

Long ago, people settled near rivers and the coast. Water provided an easy way of moving people and things, and water also has fish—it's a good source of food. People traveled by sea to explore and to trade, to fish, to seek a new place to live, and even to wage wars. Whatever the purpose of these seafarers, the sea itself was the same and presented the same challenges then as it does now. Over time, people tackled those challenges with science.

The Sea Is Wet!

The sea is liquid—that's no surprise! On land we move over solid ground and through gas (air). Much of the science of seafaring relates to moving through liquid. It deals with the properties of water and how it behaves in a large body.

What Is the Sea?

Earth's surface is divided into land and sea. The whole surface has a rocky crust, but low-lying areas are flooded with water, forming oceans and seas. Inland, dips fill with water to make lakes, rivers, and pools. People soon found traveling by sea is very different from crossing inland waters. The sea has tides, currents, and waves, and it's very easy to get lost at sea.

Sea level is not important out in the ocean, but harbors and ports are affected by changes in sea level. If sea level rises, the coast floods. If it falls, a harbor can be left dry.

Defining Sea Level

All the world's oceans are joined. That means the water level naturally evens out. When we measure elevations (heights) or depths, we can use sea level as the base, counting the surface of the sea as zero.

Where sea level is depends on how much water there is. As climate change melts ice, the extra water runs into the oceans and the sea level rises, flooding low-lying coast.

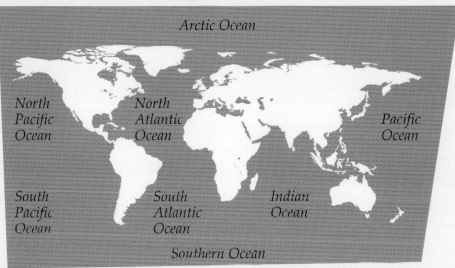

Arctic Ocean

North Pacific Ocean

North Atlantic Ocean

Pacific Ocean

South Pacific Ocean

South Atlantic Ocean

Indian Ocean

Southern Ocean

Try It Yourself

Use modeling clay to make a combined landscape and seascape with mountains, valleys, holes, and channels of different depths. Carefully pour water over your landscape; the deepest areas fill first, and the surface of the water is always flat.

Guided by the Sky

Sailors used a sextant to measure the angle between the Sun and the horizon when the Sun is highest in the sky. This shows latitude—the position between the North and South Poles.

Longitude is the position of a place measured in degrees north or south of the equator.

Where Now?

Seafarers need to know where they are, where they're going, and how to get there. Maps help near the shore, but there are no landmarks at sea. Seafarers need other methods to navigate out of sight of land. They use coordinates of latitude and longitude to give positions.

Now I know where we are!

Setting a Course

A compass shows which way is north. Using it with a map and doing some math, sailors figure out how far to turn a ship, setting a course to where they want to go.

Currents and wind can push a ship off course. Sailors need to plan for them when setting a course. They need to keep taking bearings (checking their position) and adjusting their course so they don't get lost.

Navigation by Satellite

Modern ships can use GPS to navigate even in dark and fog. A GPS system sends radio waves from satellites in orbit above Earth to a receiver on a ship to pinpoint the ship's exact position.

Fascinating Fact

Micronesian sailors sailed thousands of miles over the Pacific Ocean using maps of currents made from sticks and shells. The sticks show where currents are, and the shells are islands.

Poles and Punts

In shallow water, a boat called a punt can be pushed along using a pole that reaches to the riverbed or seabed. Pushing backward on the pole moves the boat forward.

Moving Along

The point of seafaring is to move. There are many ways of moving a ship including muscle power, sail (wind), and engines driving propellers. The earliest boats and ships were moved by human effort—people rowing, using a pole, or just paddling. Sailing boats use the wind to push the boat through the water, while mechanical methods move the water to push the boat forward. A boat can even be pedaled, like a bike! Many modern boats and ships are driven by motors powered by fuel, electricity, or even sunlight.

A hovercraft has propellers in the air rather than the water. They work by moving air to create areas of high and low pressure so that the craft moves forward.

This is good exercise!

In a boat with several rowers, the oars must work together to move the water effectively. Otherwise, the oars create lots of little currents competing against each other.

Heave Ho, Me Hearties

Moving a large Viking ship by muscle power took lots of people! They sat low in the boat and worked oars on both sides, moving in time. Oars create an area of low pressure in front of the oar and high pressure behind it. The boat is pulled forward as water moves into the area of low pressure.

Around and Around

A propeller looks somewhat like a fan, with blades attached to a shaft. An engine drives the shaft to turn the propeller in the water. Water flows over the airfoil shape of the blades, creating an area of low pressure in front of the propeller. Higher pressure behind the propeller pushes the boat forward. To turn the boat right or left, the propeller is moved in the opposite direction. Water is pushed away from where the sailor wants the boat to go, creating low pressure on that side.

Engine

Propeller

Shaft

Water flows behind the propeller

Area of low pressure in front of the propeller

Fascinating Fact

Early ships used lots of muscle power. Galleys were often rowed by slaves and, later, sailing ships often used press-ganged (kidnapped) men, since not enough people wanted to lead the grim life of a sailor.

11

Fast and Furious

A streamlined shape helps a boat cut through the water with as little drag as possible. With a pointed front end and a blunt back end, water flows around the hull smoothly.

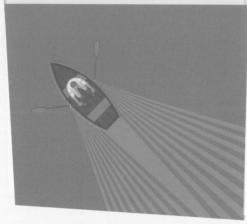

Shipshape

How a boat or ship behaves in the water depends on the shape of its hull (the bottom of the boat). The shape affects how fast it goes, how strong it is, how the forces of drag and lift act on it, and its buoyancy (ability to float). Ships are designed to suit the way they will be used. Most boats have either a U-shaped hull or a V-shaped hull.

Drag is the force that holds something back as it tries to move through a fluid, such as water or air.

Strong and Stable

A broad, round-bottomed boat (U-shaped hull) is the most stable. It's less likely to tip over than a narrow, taller boat. It's also less likely to sink, since its weight is spread over a wider area. A boat with a V-shaped hull rides higher in the waves. It's more easily tossed around by the waves, making for a bumpy ride. Cruise ships are U-shaped: They're slow, but stable and comfortable.

Inside, the hull is split into sections by watertight dividers called bulkheads. If the hull is cracked or broken, water can't flood through the entire hull. Big ships have a double-layered hull to make it difficult for anything to break right through it.

Below the Waterline

Wind →

Ships have a keel—a strong rib at the bottom of the hull that makes the boat stable. The keel can run the full length of the hull or along just part of it (called a fin keel). Sailing boats often have a deep protruding keel. It makes the boat more stable when the wind blows from the side. It's hard for the wind to tip the boat over if a large keel has to be pushed sideways through the water.

← *Keel resistance*

Fascinating Fact

Barnacles growing on the hull of a ship make it less streamlined and slow it down. Wooden ships had to stop frequently for defouling—removing barnacles, weed, and anything else clogging up the hull. Modern boats can use special antifouling paint that prevents things from sticking to the hull in the first place.

When the Wind Blows

What Wind Is

Wind is moving air. It exerts pressure (pushes) on a surface, such as a sail. The pressure can be used to move a boat along.

arly ships used sails and were pushed by the force of the wind. Modern yachts still use sails. Sails are curved to "catch" the wind and its energy. They are movable so that sailors can control the direction of the force provided by the wind, using it to drive the boat forward along the path they want to take rather than just following the wind.

When wind blows from behind the boat into the sail, it pushes the boat forward. But it's rare that the ship needs to go in the direction the wind is blowing! Sailors have to work with the wind to control the path of a ship.

14

Sailing Across the Wind

The wind flows over the surface of the sail, just as it flows over the wing of an airplane. When wind comes from the side, the force it creates pushes the boat forward and sideways. The rudder and keel stop the boat from moving sideways, so it goes forward.

Wind direction

Sail

Sailing Into the Wind

With the edge of the sail facing the wind, the sail acts like an airplane wing. The sail is lined up with the midline of the boat, front to back. The boat goes the slowest when sailing into the wind.

Wind direction

Sail

The wind is not a straightforward force going in one direction. It's full of gusts and eddies. Seabirds take advantage of these, rising and falling to make the most use of the air to carry them.

Fascinating Fact

Sailing ships could take 100 days to travel from America to Australia. With no fridges or freezers to store fresh fruit and vegetables, lots of sailors suffered from scurvy, a disease caused by lack of vitamin C. Limes and lemons helped keep them healthy.

Dirty Power

Many large ships are powered by diesel engines. The engine burns diesel and uses the pressure of the gas produced to drive the propeller shaft. The engines use cheaper, poor quality fuel that makes a lot of waste, polluting the air and sea.

Moving heavy ships through water is difficult. The top speed they can reach is about 35 miles per hour (55 kilometers per hour).

Full Steam Ahead

Ship propellers don't turn fast, like airplane propellers. They move the water by brute force, and water puts up a fight—the propellers face a lot of resistance. Modern powered ships use diesel engines, gas turbine, or electric-diesel engines to provide the force that turns the propeller shaft.

Stop!

Heavy ships can't stop quickly. Putting the propellers into reverse is the only way to slow down a large ship. It will continue moving forward long after the engines are turned off.

Electricity

New ships often use gas or diesel to generate electricity rather than to drive the ship directly. Fuel is burned in compressed air, producing hot exhaust gases. These pass over and drive a turbine, generating electricity. The electricity is then used to drive the propellers. Ships use electricity for lots of other things, too: computers for operating the ship, lighting, cooking, and entertainment. An extra supply is often produced by a separate generator.

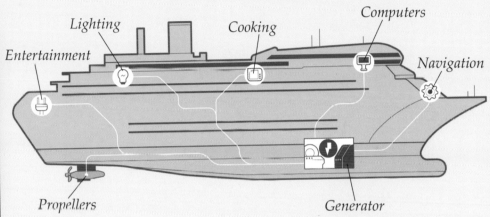

Entertainment   *Lighting*   *Cooking*   *Computers*   *Navigation*

Propellers   *Generator*

Why It Works

The rudder is used to turn the ship. Moving the rudder to the left or right uses the force of water to turn the ship in the opposite direction. A flap at the end of some rudders increases the sideways force.

Ships need lots of fuel; they carry a lot, and have to refuel at ports along the way. Fuel is delivered to them by refueling barges. Ships can go slower to use less fuel.

17

Feeling Buoyant

Buoyancy is the force of water pushing upward on an object in the water. The force is equal to the weight of the water the object has displaced (pushed aside). The forces pushing downward (the weight of the object) and upward are equal.

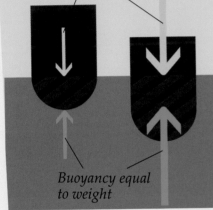

Weight of object

Buoyancy equal to weight

An object put into water displaces a volume of water equal to the volume of the part of the object that is below water.

Staying Afloat

A solid object sinks or floats depending on its density—its mass divided by its volume. If its density is greater than the density of water, it will sink; if it is less than the density of water, it will float. But a material denser than water can be made to float if it's the right shape. A ship is made of metal, which is denser than water, but ships don't usually sink. Objects are held up in the water by a force called buoyancy. In general, less dense things have more buoyancy.

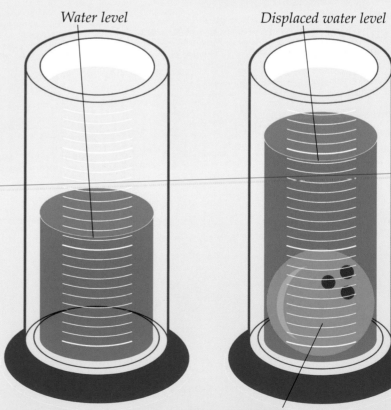

Water level

Displaced water level

Dense sunken object displacing water

Why a Metal Ship Floats

A ship is hollow—the heavy metal hull encloses a space filled with light air. Its average density is much less than the density of a lump of metal the same size. Loading cargo into the empty space makes the ship denser, so it sits lower in the water.

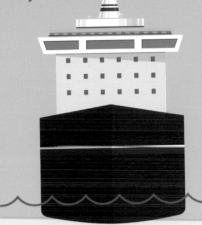

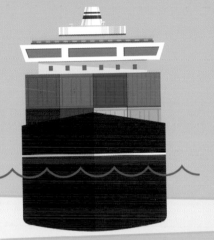

How stable something is depends on where its center of gravity lies. That's the point at which there is as much mass above as below. The lower the center of gravity, the harder it is to push an object over—including a ship.

Don't Fall!

Since a high center of gravity makes a ship less stable, it's wise to keep heavy stuff low down in a ship. A ship uses ballast (heavy material) to keep the center of gravity low if it doesn't have much to carry. The ballast is often water. Putting extra water in a ship keeps it from capsizing!

Why It Works

The Plimsoll line is a line painted on the side of a ship that shows how far up the water can safely come.

It's determined from the mass of the ship and the safe buoyancy level for it in different types of water.

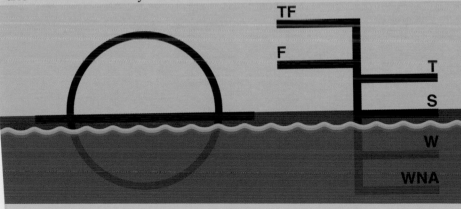

TF
F
T
S
W
WNA

TF: Tropical fresh water
F: Fresh water
T: Tropical seawater

S: Summer temperate seawater
W: Winter temperate seawater
WNA: Winter North Atlantic

See page 25 for more on why the safe water level varies for different kinds of water.

Carried Away

Trash dumped in the sea is brought together by currents and collects in huge floating patches. Trash is dangerous to sea life.

If you drop something into a moving stream, it will be carried by the current. Currents are moving water. In the sea, currents are complex. The tides, wind, and water at different pressures and temperatures work together to produce them. Surface currents work in the top 328 feet (100 meters) of water and are driven mostly by wind. Seafarers need to understand and work with currents to make efficient progress and avoid disaster. Strong currents can be very dangerous.

I wish I hadn't said you could take the boat for a spin!

Wind and Waves

Wind blows over the surface of the water producing waves. How the waves and flow of water interact with the seabed and shape of the coast produces currents. In open sea, wind systems and the rotation of Earth combine to produce complex currents.

Time and Tide

The pull of the Moon's gravity acts on the water of Earth's oceans, helping to create the pattern of the tides. As Earth turns on its axis every 24 hours, and the Moon moves slowly around Earth, the tides follow a pattern that is roughly daily, but shifting by a few a minutes each day.

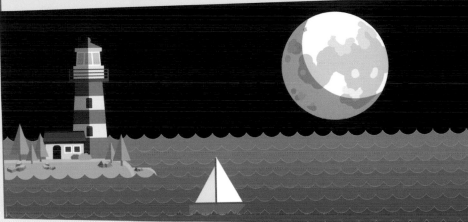

Can You Believe It?

A shipping accident in 1992 released 28,000 plastic ducks into the sea. Scientists have learned a lot about ocean currents from tracking where the ducks are carried.

Wildlife relies on ocean currents. Changes in the currents, probably caused by climate change, killed off 95 percent of all types of marine life 252 million years ago.

Deep-Ocean Currents

A long-term pattern of movement of water around the world is driven by the different densities of warm and cold water. Over 1,000 years, water makes a complete circuit through the Atlantic and Pacific Oceans, and goes from the surface to the seabed. It's carried by predictable deep-ocean currents, traveling at about an inch (a few centimeters) per second.

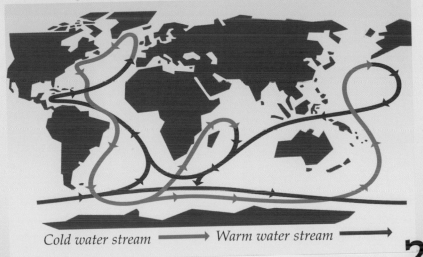

Cold water stream → Warm water stream →

21

Waves and Wavelength

Many types of energy move in waves, including sound, light, and radio.

Seafarers have to understand waves to be safe on the water. Waves represent energy. As you watch a wave coming to the shore and breaking, what you're seeing is the effect of the movement of energy on water. Surfers use the energy of breaking waves to have fun, but large waves can be dangerous to ships and boats.

Surfing is so much fun!

Up and Down

Wave direction

Crest falling

Trough rising

Water particles move in circles as the wave of energy passes through the water, creating the rising and falling wavy surface. Each water particle travels only half the distance of the wavelength (from one wave peak to the next).

A wave breaks when its amplitude (height) becomes too great. The wave energy is turned into kinetic (movement) energy. The crest of the wave falls over and the water moves wildly.

Breaking Point

The distance between waves and the length of a ship are important. On rough seas, the ends of the ship might be supported by waves, but the middle might not. Or a wave under the middle might leave the ends unsupported. A boat can break apart when only some of it is supported by water.

Steady as She Goes

Rolling with the waves makes people seasick, and can tip cargo overboard. Stabilizers help to keep a ship steady. They can be fins that stick out at the sides of the hull, or tanks of water that move side to side as the ship rocks, counteracting the action of the swell.

Stabilizers

Fascinating Fact

Gulp! Has it been 10,000 years already?

For a long time, rogue waves of 98 feet (30 m) or more were dismissed as exaggeration or myth. That's because hardly anyone who saw one survived. Then, in 1995, a system designed to survive a wave size expected only once every 10,000 years measured one larger than the predicted 10,000-year wave—after just 11 years!

Salt Water and Fresh Water

Salt water has a higher density than fresh water, which is why it's easier to float in the sea than in a river or swimming pool. Salt water also freezes at a lower temperature than fresh water, at about 28.4 degrees Fahrenheit (-2 degrees Celsius). This means the sea temperature can fall below freezing point without actually freezing over.

We can't drink seawater. Lifeboats carry fresh water and have systems for removing the salt from seawater.

The Salty Sea

The sea is salty, with dissolved sodium chloride and small amounts of other minerals. By some estimates, if the salt in the ocean could be removed and spread evenly over Earth's land surface it would form a layer more than 500 feet (152 m) thick, about the height of a 40-story office building. Salt water doesn't have the same properties as fresh water and behaves differently, too. Seafarers need to take this into account since it affects boats and how they respond to the water.

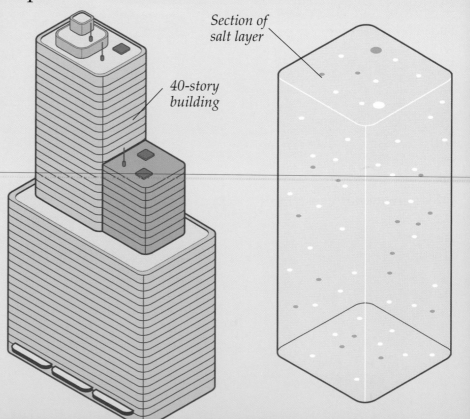

Section of salt layer

40-story building

Hot and Cold

Buoyancy varies with water temperature. Cold water is denser than hot water, so a boat loaded in a cold place will lie lower in the water when it sails to warmer seas. But the density of ice is lower than the density of cold water, so icebergs float.

Water expands as it freezes, so a ship trapped in ice can be crushed. As water around the ship freezes, it takes up more space, pressing harder and harder against the hull.

Built to Last

Salt water damages ships, whether they are made of wood or metal. For 600 years, sailors used tar to protect wood and rigging on sailing ships. Today, wooden boats are protected with epoxy resin. Metal hulls are dotted with plates called "sacrificial anodes" made of zinc. Seawater attacks zinc in preference to the iron of the ship. The plates have to be frequently checked and replaced when they become corroded.

Try It Yourself

Make a "boat" from a plastic carton, and put a few things in it. Set your boat in a bowl of water and mark where the water comes to on the side. Dissolve a lot of salt in the water. Where does the water come to now?

25

Down in the Depths

Going Up and Going Down

Submarines take in and release air and seawater to change their buoyancy to go up or sink down.

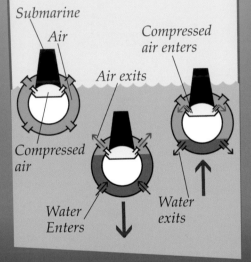

Submarine
Air
Compressed air enters
Air exits
Compressed air
Water Enters
Water exits

Most kinds of seacraft attempt to stay above the waves, but submarines sink beneath on purpose. Beneath the water, it's possible for submarines to observe other seacraft without being seen themselves. However, being underwater exposes them to different challenges and forces. These have to be taken into account in their design.

Shhh, don't make a sound!

Submarines have a double-layered hull. The strong inner hull resists the huge pressure of the water around the submarine.

Beep, Beep, Beep

Submarines use radar to navigate at the surface, and sonar to navigate under the water and to map the seabed. The military uses it to detect other ships.

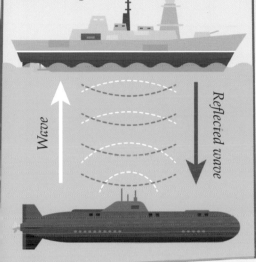

Wave

Reflected wave

Looking Around

Some types of submarines are used to investigate the deep sea. They explore the wildlife of the deep, the rocks of the seabed, and the nature of the seawater far below the surface.

These submarines may have large windows to allow observation of sea life. They may also have lightweight mechanical arms to retrieve samples from the seabed.

Viewports for observation

Lightweight mechanical arms

Sonar and radar work by sending out a beam of sound or radio waves and measuring how long the echo takes to return. The time reveals the distance to a solid object.

Can You Believe It?

Sonar mapping reveals a landscape of mountains, plains, and valleys beneath the oceans. It's vital to shipping to know where there are unseen rocks below the surface.

Coral reefs are destroyed by ships running into them and by fishing boats dragging heavy beams underwater.

Sea Life and Sustainability

The sea is full of living things. The health of the oceans is essential to the whole world, affecting the food supply, atmosphere, and weather. It's important for seafaring to be sustainable to protect the oceans. Ninety percent of the world's goods are moved by sea, using 100,000 ships and producing three percent of all greenhouse gases.

A Bit Fishy

Improved technology has made it possible for fishing boats to fish mid-ocean and in the deep sea. This has damaged fish populations —and not just of the fish we eat. Some fish are caught accidentally and not used. This is called bycatch.

All Gone to Waste

Large ships produce huge volumes of solid and liquid waste that pollutes the sea. The best, newest liners process liquid waste using ultraviolet radiation and bacteria until it's as good as seawater. They sort, crush, and store trash for recycling. But in much of the world, ships dump waste at sea, including dirty bilgewater from the tanks that keep ships stable.

Oil spills and other accidental losses from ships pollute oceans. Oil lost from tankers floats on top of the sea. It sticks to seabirds and sea mammals, wrecking the insulating feathers and fur that keeps the animals warm, and killing them.

Sustainable Seafaring

Cutting the fuel used makes seafaring more sustainable—and cheaper! Improved, cleaner engines use higher grade fuels that produce less waste. Computers calculate routes to make the best use of currents and improve planning to cut the time spent waiting to enter port with engines running. Better management of waste, using bio-friendly hull paints, and using solar or wind power all help.

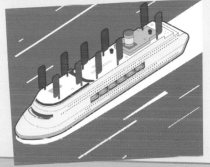

Try It Yourself

Fill a wide pan or tray with water—this is your sea. Mix gel-based food coloring or a little oil paint into some cooking oil and pour it gently onto the water. It will float on the top. Now dip a cotton ball, a piece of fabric, and a feather into the water. See how the oil coats the surface? This is what happens to seabirds in an oil spill.

Glossary

Airfoil The shape of the cross-section of fan blade, like a long teardrop.

Bacteria Microscopic living things.

Barnacle Tiny sea crustacean with a hard shell that attaches itself to a surface.

Bilgewater Water carried in the bilge tanks of a ship to keep it stable.

Bio-friendly Not damaging to the environment or living things.

Buoyancy The force that pushes upward from beneath an object in the water, keeping it afloat.

Cargo Goods carried in a ship.

Climate change Changes to long-term patterns of weather.

Compass A tool with an iron needle that always points to magnetic north

Coordinates Pair of numbers that identify a precise location.

Current The movement of a body of water (or air) in a particular direction.

Diesel A type of fuel that ignites automatically when mixed with air under pressure.

Drag The force that slows an object as it moves through water or air.

Eddy Circular movement of water, creating a small whirlpool.

Epoxy resin A substance used to make very tough varnishes and glues.

Galley A large boat driven along by banks of rowers in the hull.

Gravity The force that pulls objects with mass toward each other.

Greenhouse gas A gas high in the atmosphere that keeps Earth warm.

Hovercraft A vehicle that travels over the water on a "skirt" filled with air.

Hull The lower part of a ship or boat that sits in the water.

Lift A force that pushes upward on an object suspended in air or water.

Minerals Chemical compounds often found in rocks and in dissolved form in seawater.

Navigate To find a route to or through somewhere.

Pollute To contaminate an environment with waste.

Pressure The force produced by one surface pushing against another, or by a higher concentration of matter in one area than another.

Propeller A device that looks somewhat like a fan, with turning blades that push air or water out of the way.

Punt A flat-bottomed boat moved through shallow water with a pole.

Radar A system for finding objects in air or space by bouncing radio waves off them and measuring the time for the "echo" to return.

Radiation Energy that travels as electromagnetic waves.

Rigging The ropes that hold the sails in place on a sailing ship.

Sextant A tool used by sailors to measure the angle between the horizon and the Sun.

Sonar A system for finding objects in air or water by bouncing high-pitched sound off them and measuring the time for the echo to return.

Streamlined With a shape that allows the easy flow of water or air around it.

Turbine A machine with fan blades turned by moving liquid or gas. The energy from the turning blades can be used to make electricity for an electric engine.

Ultraviolet Type of radiation with wavelength slightly shorter than that of visible light.

Index